# Understanding *Mental* ILLNESS

## For Teens Who Care about Someone with Mental Illness

Julie Tallard Johnson

**Lerner Publications Company**

**Minneapolis**

*This edition of this book is available in two bindings:*
Library binding by Lerner Publications Company
Soft cover by First Avenue Editions
241 First Avenue North
Minneapolis, Minnesota 55401

LIBRARY OF CONGRESS CATALOGING-IN-PUBLICATION DATA

**Johnson, Julie Tallard.**
   Understanding mental illness : for teens who care about someone
with mental illness / Julie Tallard Johnson.
      p.   cm.
   Bibliography: p.
   Includes index.
   Summary: Examines the different mental illnesses and offers
assistance for those living with the mentally ill.
   ISBN 0-8225-0042-6 (lib. bdg.)
   ISBN 0-8225-9574-5 (pbk.)
   1. Mental illness—Juvenile literature. [1. Mental illness.]
I. Title.
RC460.2.J64   1989
616.89—dc19                                                    88-27129
                                                                   CIP
                                                                    AC

Manufactured in the United States of America

2  3  4  5  6  7  8  9  10  99  98  97  96  95  94  93  92  91  90

## *Acknowledgments*

I am first most grateful to those many teenagers who were willing to share their stories with me. It is through your personal openness that others will be helped.

I am grateful to Lerner Publications and Theresa Early for recognizing a need for this book, to my talented and patient editor, LeeAnne Engfer, to Anna Swanson for reading over the first draft of the book, to Jeff Cilley for his continued insights, and to my first mentor, Bev Young. All of you made this book a reality.

Finally, I am grateful to my parents, whose support and love will be found in each word of each page.

Thank you.

This book is dedicated to
my brother Rick, who understands,
and to the National Alliance for
the Mentally Ill, for being there.

# Contents

# Preface

*Understanding Mental Illness* is for teens who know or care about someone with a mental illness. You will find answers to questions you might have about the mentally ill person. You may have concerns like Rebecca, who wrote a letter asking for advice on how to deal with her brother's mental illness:

Dear Julie,

Is there anyone I can talk to who has a brother or sister with schizophrenia? The doctors tell me that my brother Stephen is schizophrenic. He had a nervous breakdown when he was 17 years old. He takes medicine, but it's not working and he doesn't always take it when he should. He drinks beer and takes street drugs. My mom gives him money, but all he spends it on is drugs and alcohol. He's never going to amount to anything if he keeps it up. He tells me he cannot concentrate. His behavior changes so fast. One moment he is friendly and makes sense. The next minute he is nasty to me.

When Stephen was a kid, he would often start fights with me. He would hit, pinch, and kick me. I'm 16 years old now. He seems real jealous of me because I am younger than him and I am finishing school but he is not. What can I do? Is something wrong with my family? What exactly is schizophrenia? Is there someone I can talk with who knows about schizophrenia? I'm afraid that I may have schizophrenia too—is this possible? Sometimes I hate my brother. I also wish he would try to get well, because sometimes he can be nice.

I hope to hear from you soon. Until now I thought I was the only one who had a brother like this.

Sincerely,

Rebecca

Rebecca has been living with her brother Stephen's illness for a long time. It wasn't until recently, though, that she and her family were told that Stephen has schizophrenia. Rebecca is relieved to discover there is a name for Stephen's problem; somehow that makes it less frightening. But she is still confused about what all this means.

You may be confused and have questions as well. What are the facts about mental illness? Just what is schizophrenia and how does a person get it? What are depression and manic depression? Is there something wrong with the family? How can you get help? Did you do anything to cause the illness? If you have a friend or relative with a mental illness, you probably have questions like these.

This book is to help you understand mental illness and what happens to families who live with this disease. It will help you understand how the mental illness of someone you love affects you. Once you begin to understand, you will start feeling better about the mentally ill person, your family, and yourself. Understanding something gives you a sense of power and peace of mind. Take the time to read this book, talk with others, and ask yourself questions. Taking the time to understand will not always be easy, but it will be worth it.

You will learn that you cannot cure someone of mental illness—or any disease—but you can make life better for yourself and those you care about. *It all begins with you.*

# CHAPTER ONE

# Facts About Mental Illness

### Sara's Brother

Sara has noticed some strange changes in her brother Eric. He seems agitated and keeps to himself a lot. He doesn't play basketball anymore. When his friends call him, he won't answer the phone. Sometimes he spends days alone in his room, coming out only after everyone is asleep. At night he wanders into Sara's room and stands next to her bed mumbling. When he's in his room alone, he talks to himself. Sara is afraid. Eric says that something awful is happening inside him. He thinks someone is trying to poison him. Sara is not sure what's wrong, but she's worried about Eric.

### Peter's Mother

Peter's mother cries a lot. Ever since she had Peter's

younger sister Jamie three years ago, his mom has seemed so unhappy and afraid. She doesn't do many of the things she used to do with Peter. Peter just turned 13. His mother would have forgotten his birthday if he hadn't reminded her. She didn't even pretend to remember it was his birthday! She just doesn't seem to care about much at all anymore. Peter's not sure what to do or who to talk to. His father seems worried too, but he doesn't talk to Peter about his mother. Peter doesn't want to go to school, he is so concerned about his sister and mother. He wonders if this is how all mothers act after having a baby. Sometimes he thinks he did something wrong to make her unhappy.

Sara's brother and Peter's mother are showing warning signs of a mental illness. Peter's mother may suffer from depression. And Sara's brother might have schizophrenia. What can they do about it? What will help them deal with such a disease?

Does someone you care about have a mental illness? Have you overheard someone saying that a person you know is "crazy"? Maybe you have a family member whom you have been told has schizophrenia or depression. You are probably curious and even frightened. What does it mean to have a mental illness?

*Mental illness is a disease of the brain that affects how someone feels, thinks, and behaves.*

The term "mental illness" is used to describe a

variety of brain diseases. The words mental illness are often misunderstood. Sometimes people misuse the word "mental" to describe someone they think is "bad," "stupid," or "evil." But mentally ill people aren't bad or evil; they have a disease. They are in pain.

Perhaps you have heard that a family member or friend has **schizophrenia** or **manic depression**. Schizophrenia, depression, and manic depression are the most common mental illnesses. Other mental illnesses include autism, personality disorders, and agoraphobia.

Knowing something about these diseases can help you understand why people with mental illness behave the way they do, and what might help them get better.

**Agoraphobia** is one of the more common **phobias**. A phobia is an intense and irrational fear of something. Only when the fear is *persistent* and *intense* is it considered a phobia. Agoraphobia is an abnormal fear of being in public places. Someone with agoraphobia may remain shut in his or her home for years.

**Autism** is a disease primarily identified in children. Children with autism appear unresponsive and uninterested in other people. They often have slurred speech or do not speak at all. Children with autism may have a strong attachment to a toy or some other object. They do not usually play with other children, and they act in ways that don't relate to what is going on around them. Autistic children appear not to understand what is happening around them, although they can be very intelligent. Autism is considered a brain disease that occurs in a child before she or he is one month old.

**Personality disorders** is a term that covers a wide range of disorders, including borderline personality disorder, antisocial disorder, and narcissistic disorder. Often people with these disorders are dramatic, disruptive, and anxious, and at times they physically hurt themselves or others. However, each disease has its own set of characteristics. If you know someone who has been described as having a personality disorder, you may want to find out more about the specific disorder by asking your family doctor or a school psychologist.

**Schizophrenia** is considered a brain disease. Symptoms include impaired, mixed-up thinking, severe changes in emotion—or no show of emotion—hearing voices that aren't there, and severe changes in behavior. The disease interferes with one's ability to interpret his or her surroundings accurately.

People with schizophrenia and other mentally ill people are not *mentally retarded*. In fact, many persons with schizophrenia or other mental illnesses are very intelligent.

**Depression** is a disease that causes someone to experience intense and persistent feelings of sadness.

**Manic depression** is a disease that causes someone to swing between times of feeling extreme sadness to feeling all right to times of intense energy and enthusiasm.

The specific types of mental illness differ, but they

all interfere with how someone feels, thinks, and acts. They disturb not only the lives of the persons with the disease, but the lives of those who care about them.

At times all of us experience intense feelings, such as grief, fear, or excitement. It is common and normal to have strong feelings. It is also true that we all have peculiar thoughts about ourselves and others sometimes. The important difference is that people with a mental illness have intense emotions and confused thoughts which are *persistent,* many times *unpredictable,* and often *unrelated* to outside circumstances. In contrast to a healthy individual, someone with a mental illness may be depressed for weeks or months, without change and without any apparent reason. You may feel very sad and angry after losing a sweater you received as a gift, but you do not continue to feel sad for weeks, months, or a year. The sadness you experience is also predictable, because it relates to a particular circumstance (losing your sweater).

People who have a mental illness often act strangely. Those who live with or are close to the mentally ill are affected by their peculiar, sometimes frightening, behavior. If your parent, brother, sister, friend, aunt, uncle, or other relative has a mental illness, their disease affects *you.* This doesn't mean you can catch it—mental illness is not contagious. But caring about someone with a mental illness isn't easy. Sometimes you are frightened for them or yourself. You may worry about them. Someone else's disease affects how *you* feel.

## *You Are Not Alone*

Sharing a home with someone who has a mental illness is difficult—and much more common than you may think. At least *one in four* families has a member with a serious mental illness like schizophrenia or depression. More hospital beds are used by people with a mental illness than by people with any other disease. More than 20 million U.S. citizens will have an episode of depression or manic depression during their lifetime. Approximately 8 million children under the age of 18 have some kind of mental illness or serious problem adjusting to life.

This means that *you are not alone.* Other people understand exactly what you are going through, because they have had similar experiences. Someone you know probably has a family member or a friend with a serious mental illness. They have felt confused, frightened, embarrassed, angry, and worried, just like you. They have learned how to live with someone else's mental illness while still enjoying their own lives. You can too.

## *Mental Illness Is a Disease*

Like arthritis, diabetes, or cancer, mental illness is a disease. Unlike most diseases, which show physical symptoms, mental illness expresses itself through **behaviors** and **moods**. Because mental illnesses are brain diseases, they affect how people *think* and interpret what's going on around them.

For someone with schizophrenia, for example, it

becomes difficult to distinguish fantasy from reality. The most obvious sign of schizophrenia is that the schizophrenic person's mind "plays tricks" on him. This can happen in two ways. One way is that the person's senses are confused—he may hear voices, see things, or smell odors that aren't really there. These "tricks" on the senses are called **hallucinations**. That's why you might see schizophrenic people talking to themselves—they are often talking back to the voices they hear.

The second trick the schizophrenic person's mind plays is when she begins to believe things that aren't true. We call these beliefs **delusions**. Delusions are fixed ideas held despite logical proof against them. Delusions may cause someone to believe she is somebody she is not, or to think a fantasy is real when it is not. People with schizophrenia often act nervous, suspicious, and angry because they have delusions that frighten them.

Mental illness can also affect how someone *feels*. Characteristics of depression, for example, include feeling despair, hopelessness, and fear. Most people with depression feel very lonely, sad, and frightened if they are not being treated with medication or by counseling. They often keep to themselves because they don't have enough energy to interact with other people.

People's behavior is consistent with how they think and feel. A person who *thinks* she is a rock star *behaves* like a rock star. Someone who *feels* depressed *acts* depressed. Many people with mental illness act and feel afraid. This is because they really believe there is something to be afraid of. Most of the time the voices schizophrenic people hear are saying frightening things, for example.

Another common characteristic of people with mental illness is that they assume that much of what goes on around them happens especially for them or because of them. One young man, Kurt, became depressed at the age of 16. When things didn't go right, Kurt felt responsible. He once commented, "My bad mood causes storms."

Kurt's moods can't actually cause storms. But often people with mental illness—especially when they aren't being treated—believe such things.

Often the mentally ill person denies he has a problem. Sometimes he blames others for how he feels or what he thinks. Perhaps you have been blamed for someone's unhappiness. But you are not to blame; no one is to blame. The mentally ill person may believe that others caused his problem, but no one should be held responsible for giving someone else mental illness. *Mental illness is a disease, and no one is to blame.*

## *What Causes Mental Illness?*

No one knows for certain what causes mental illness. There are many theories, however. Recent research suggests that three factors *together* may contribute to mental illness.

• **Chemical/Biological Imbalance**

One belief is that mental illness is caused by a chemical or biological imbalance in the brain. Chemicals, cells, molecules, and tissues in our bodies interact to keep us healthy. According to this belief, mentally ill people have a serious biological imbalance in their brains, which causes them to be "off balance," much like a car running low on oil. The car's system is "off balance" and will break down if the problem isn't fixed.

Our brains are delicate and far more complex than a car's engine. To understand all the information we receive each moment, our brains must be functioning properly. **Neurotransmitters** are an important part of our brain's operation. Neurotransmitters are the biological substances in the brain which transmit (move) nerve impulses, carrying messages from one nerve cell to another. These messages make contact by way of a **synapse**. The synapse joins the nerve cells, allowing the nerve impulse to pass from cell to cell.

In someone with schizophrenia, for example, the synapses might not be working properly; they do not allow the right "message" (impulse) to be sent from cell to cell. As a result, the person receives an inaccurate message. This explains why a person with schizophrenia may behave in a bizarre or unpredictable way. This person is simply responding to the inaccurate message that his brain is giving him.

• **Genetic Makeup**

Another important theory is that mental illness is

hereditary. This means that some mental illnesses run in families—they are passed down from generation to generation. We are each born with a certain genetic makeup—a set of genes and chromosomes that determines what we will be like. Our genes dictate our hair and eye color, for example, and they influence how thin or fat and tall or short we are. People with a mental illness may have a defective gene or set of genes which increases their chance of having a mental illness. Many studies show that genes and chromosomes contribute to the development of a mental illness. Different mental illnesses may be caused by different defective genes. Genetic researchers continue to discover more evidence of this.

Just because a mental illness is inherited does not mean it is incurable. Many inherited diseases, including mental illness, can be cured with proper treatment.

### • Serious External Stresses

Serious external stresses, such as physical or sexual abuse, taking street drugs like LSD, speed, or crack, drinking too much alcohol, serious head injuries, or the death of a loved one, can contribute to the onset of a mental illness. Many families report that a family member's mental illness first occurred when the person suffered an injury to the head, was experimenting with street drugs, or suffered extreme stress like a death in the family. One young person became ill with schizophrenia shortly after a motorcycle accident in which he wasn't wearing a helmet. Some people think that complications during pregnancy or birth may increase the chance of a person getting a mental illness.

Whatever the cause or causes, we do know that there is something that definitely did not cause the mental illness—*you.*

## *What* Doesn't *Cause Mental Illness?*

Although all the specific causes of mental illnesses are not precisely known, it *is* certain that mental illness is not caused by:

- "sinful" behavior
- possession by evil spirits
- laziness
- poor parenting
- peer pressure
- too much television
- poor sibling (sister or brother) relationships

A person doesn't have a mental illness because he or she is a bad person. Even if mentally ill people act "bad" or frightening, they are not bad people. The disease often prevents them from feeling good and acting nice. This does not mean it is all right for the person to hurt or threaten you. Mental illness is not an excuse for someone to be abusive. The disease does, however, influence how a person thinks and behaves—and often the behavior is unfriendly or nasty.

*It is not that the mentally ill person doesn't love or care for you. The disease prevents him or her from expressing those feelings.*

When people become ill, their lives change. The disease prevents mentally ill people from doing everything the way they want to; they just aren't able to do some things. A person who is born without a leg probably can't run a marathon or dance as well as people with two legs. But people with physical handicaps learn to live with their limitations. People with mental illness also can learn to live with their disease.

## Treatment of Mental Illness

Many treatment programs are available for people with a mental illness. Below are some of the common forms of treatment. For further information, refer to the *Where to Go for Help* section at the back of the book.

• **Drug Therapy, Medications**

Drugs are usually administered to a person with mental illness by a physician, typically a psychiatrist. Medications for mental illness are called **psychotropics**, and there are hundreds of different kinds. What kind of medication a person takes depends on the particular mental illness. For example, when someone is diagnosed as having schizophrenia, he or she is often given a medication called Prolixin. But it is only one of many that could be given to someone with schizophrenia. Lithium is usually given to those with manic depression, and there are dozens of drugs for depression.

Medications allow people's bodies and brains to work better so they can live a more normal life. When someone is on medication, disabling symptoms such as depression, hearing voices, or fearing public places often disappear. Many people with schizophrenia need to remain on medication for a lifetime, while people with depression may only need medication during especially low times. Because the use of medication is such a complex and personal issue, the choice of which drug to take is ultimately decided by the doctor and the person who needs the medication.

## • Community Treatment

Community treatment for those with mental illness includes adult foster homes, day treatment programs, case management, drop-in centers, and community mental health centers. Most of these programs are offered in various places in the community and are available to any adult with a mental illness. There are also community programs for teens who have a mental illness. To find out what is available in your community, contact the local Alliance for the Mentally Ill or the Mental Health Association.

## • Hospitalization

"Hospitalization" refers to the time someone spends in a hospital for treatment. *Short-term* hospitalization occurs after a crisis or when an individual cannot take care of herself without a lot of attention. Usually, the person stays in the hospital until she is able to care for herself. The length of stay varies from 24 hours to about 3 weeks. These hospitalizations generally take place in a local public, private, or university hospital.

Another kind of hospitalization is *long-term*, ranging from several weeks to several years. This type of hospitalization is necessary only for those who are incapable of living in the community due to the disabling symptoms of their mental illness. Sometimes hospitals where long-term patients stay are referred to as state hospitals, but they can be public or private as well. These hospitals are usually located outside the community and only serve people who have mental illnesses or other serious mental health problems.

To be hospitalized, an adult must either choose to go in or must go through a legal procedure which proves that the person is better off getting treatment in the hospital than in the community. This procedure is called a "commitment." A judge decides if the person needs to be in the hospital or not.

Social workers at either type of hospital can answer your questions about what kind of treatment and help they offer their patients. The social workers may not be able to answer specific questions about your friend or family member. Social workers and other hospital staff cannot tell you everything about their patients, because that is private information. But they can answer many of your questions. Simply call the hospital and ask for the social worker who helps your family member or friend. Be persistent. Hospital social workers are very busy, but they are there to help you, too.

• **Counseling**
A variety of counseling services are available to people with mental illness and their families. One-to-one counseling usually takes place with a psychologist, social worker, or some other professional therapist. Counseling can also take place in a therapy group with others who have common problems. For people with schizophrenia, supportive problem-solving counseling seems to be most effective. Counseling for families of the mentally ill can help them deal with how mental illness has affected them. To find a counselor or therapy group, call your local mental health center.

## Don't Take It upon Yourself to Cure Someone of Mental Illness

One day Jessica climbed a large oak tree with her friend Kathy. From the top they could see down the hill to the street where some friends lived. As they reached the top, it began to pour, and the branches quickly got dark and slippery. As Kathy tried to climb down, she fell. She lay unconscious on the ground for a long time. Jessica held on tightly to the branch until some neighborhood people heard her cries for help and helped her down with a ladder. She now feels guilty, because Kathy is in a body cast and her right arm might be permanently damaged. Jessica thinks she should have tried harder to climb down, and she should have gotten help for her friend. She feels sad and guilty for holding on to the branch. Sometimes she even wishes she had fallen instead of Kathy.

Like Jessica, at times we feel responsible and guilty when someone we care about is hurt. Do you sometimes feel guilty because you are healthy while someone you care about has a mental illness? Most of us who care about a mentally ill person have thoughts like these at times. But *you are not responsible for someone else's disease or behavior.* You did not cause someone else's mental illness. You are not responsible for curing it. Nothing you alone can do can cure the mentally ill person. It was good that Jessica held onto the branch until help came. Otherwise both girls might now be in body casts.

All we can really do is try to understand and love the mentally ill person, and live our own lives. It is all right to feel good about yourself and to take care of yourself the best you can, even when your friend or relative has a disease.

# CHAPTER TWO

# Understanding the Mentally Ill Person

People with mental illness show symptoms of their disease, just like people with chicken pox get red spots and people with epilepsy have convulsions. Symptoms of mental illness include mood swings, mixed-up thoughts, inconsistent behavior, intense fear and anxiety, and hallucinations.

Often the mentally ill cannot control how they behave. Understanding the symptoms of the common mental illnesses described below may help you understand someone you know who is mentally ill.

## *Understanding Depression*

### Lisa's Mom

Ever since Lisa's father died three years ago, Lisa's mom doesn't seem to be involved in much. She no longer goes for the walks she and Lisa used to take every Saturday. Lisa began getting worried about her mother about two years after her father died. She tried talking to her brother, but he didn't want to talk about it. Lisa's aunt said her mother's behavior was normal—she just missed her husband and would get over it in time. But Lisa wasn't so sure—after all, she missed her dad too.

Finally, Lisa talked to her school counselor, who suggested Lisa visit her family doctor. At Lisa's yearly checkup, she told the doctor what was happening at home. The doctor asked Lisa's mother to come in for a checkup. He found out that Lisa's mother has depression. The doctor got Lisa's mother in touch with a counselor who helps people with depression. Lisa's mother is now in a group for people who are trying to recover from depression, and she takes medicine that helps her feel better.

Now life at home has improved. Lisa's mother doesn't do all the things she used to do, but she's much more active and happier than she was before she went to the counselor. Lisa hopes her mom will go for a walk with her Saturday, but she realizes that her mom may not be ready for that quite yet.

Many people who are depressed lack energy. They say it feels like they are walking through sand on a very humid day. Their feelings of sadness are extreme and constant. People with depression are often withdrawn and uninterested in what once made them happy.

Depressed people don't always feel lonely, weak, and unhappy. As with many diseases, mental illness has cycles. Someone suffering from depression moves from feeling OK to feeling despondent. The right medication and treatment can interrupt the cycle, allowing the person to feel good for longer periods.

People who are depressed often isolate themselves. For them even the simplest task requires too much energy. When they isolate themselves, they become more depressed and negative, sometimes acting hostile and irritable toward others. They lack the energy and ideas that could help them overcome their depression. Decisions are difficult for them and everyday responsibilities sometimes become impossible.

Long periods of depression can lead people to wish they were dead and to think about killing themselves.

**Someone you know may have depression if he or she:**
- has difficulty concentrating
- does not want to talk with you or others
- no longer participates in activities he or she used to enjoy
- sleeps too little or too much
- talks negatively about self and others
- has a poor appetite, which may show in a rapid loss of weight. Sometimes the person may have an increased appetite, which shows in rapid weight gain
- is more irritable toward you and others

- feels hopeless about the future
- cries easily
- talks about death or suicide

These are not necessarily signs of a mental illness. But if these behaviors are **severe**, **persistent**, or **recurrent**, professional help is needed.

**Severe** describes a behavior that is more harsh and intense in response to an event than the event warrants. The behavior is often viewed as an overreaction to a situation. For example, where you might feel scared, a mentally ill person may experience paranoia, an intense and severe fear. A person suffering from paranoia might lock himself in his room because he hears sirens outside. A **persistent** behavior continues over a long period of time. It also occurs in a variety of different settings, like home, school, and while visiting relatives. Someone who is *always* afraid of others, no matter where he is, is showing a persistent behavior. **Recurrent** describes a behavior which *reappears* or is repeated. Recurrent behaviors can be predictable ("My dad gets depressed every spring and fall") or they may be less predictable ("I never know when my sister is going to start yelling and pacing again").

*There is help for people with depression.* Books, medications, counseling, and organizations are available to help those who suffer from depression. You may want to call your local mental health center for information. Most telephone books list mental health services and emergency numbers. You may also want to talk to your school counselor.

We can offer our love, ideas, and resources to those in pain, but we can't make them feel better or force them to get help. It is just as important to get help for yourself. Lisa attends a special group after school that teaches her about her mother's disease. The group is offered through the school and is made up of other teenagers who have relatives with a mental illness. Another girl her age also has a mother with depression, and since joining the group they have become good friends.

## Understanding Manic Depression

### Why Does Your Dad Talk So Fast?

The other day, Johnnie and his best friend Aaron were visiting in Johnnie's bedroom. Suddenly Johnnie's father came in and began talking about model airplanes, aerodynamics, space travel, aliens, and various inventions he was working on in the garage. Johnnie started to feel embarrassed and angry. "Why did my dad come in, anyway?" he thought. "He wasn't invited and he didn't even knock." Johnnie could tell that Aaron was puzzled by his dad's behavior, but Aaron was curious to see what Johnnie's father was working on in the garage.

Before Aaron could ask to see the inventions, however, Johnnie's father had started telling them that he was going to write letters to the government about putting more money into space projects. He disappeared down the hallway, still talking. When he was gone, Aaron asked Johnnie, "Why does your dad talk so fast?"

Johnnie isn't sure, but he has seen his dad get that way many times. He considers his dad to be moody and unpredictable. Just last week, he was withdrawn and wouldn't talk to anyone, but today nobody can get him to be quiet. Most of the time, Johnnie worries about his dad, but that day he wished he could run and hide from Aaron's questions.

Many famous people are believed to have had manic depression—people like Patty Duke, the actress, Abraham Lincoln, the president, Ernest Hemingway, the writer, and Vincent van Gogh, the painter.

A person with manic depression often swings between feeling very high, excited, and ambitious to feeling very low, immobile, and withdrawn. The depression part of manic depression is the same as having the kind of depression described earlier. The difference is that people with manic depression also are **manic** at times.

During the manic period, the person experiences a sense of creativity and intense energy. Many experts believe that some of the world's greatest writers, performers, and artists have had manic depression. Their creative energy peaked during the manic part of their cycle.

The intensity of energy and creativity often becomes

unbearable for family and friends—and for the person with the illness. For most people, manic episodes do not result in a creative endeavor like a book or a movie, but in a disaster. Many people spend money they don't have, act dangerously, or believe they have powers that they do not possess. One woman believed she was a messenger of God. Consequently, she preached on the street to passersby and soon after ended up in the hospital.

Famous people with manic depression suffered too. Ernest Hemingway and Vincent van Gogh committed suicide, and Patty Duke wrote a book about her difficult fight against the disease.

**Someone you know may have manic depression if he or she:**
- swings between periods of feeling extreme sadness to feeling all right to times of intense energy and enthusiasm

**Someone may be having a *manic* period when he or she:**
- has a noticeable and continuous increase in energy
- does not sleep for very many hours and still has a lot of energy
- speaks very rapidly and is excited about many ideas
- talks a lot about God (especially if he or she did not often mention God before). The person often believes he or she has a special relationship with God.
- has a decrease in appetite

- cannot control his or her behavior
- shares strange and new ideas about self and the world

Help is available for people with manic depression. With the right medication and support, most people with this disease live happy, productive lives. Because Johnnie's father hasn't seen a doctor for over 10 years, no one has identified his behavior—his mood swings—as manic depression. Until his illness is identified, Johnnie's father won't be able to get help.

There are groups across the country for people who have depression or manic depression. These groups also offer help to family and friends. Refer to the resource list at the back of the book and contact the national headquarters for the group closest to you. Discover that you are not alone and that help is available.

## Understanding Schizophrenia

### Jenny's Aunt Vivian

It's not that Jenny doesn't like her Aunt Vivian. She does—*sometimes.* Aunt Vivian can be funny. Her skin is all stretchy and she makes faces by pulling her skin around. But she talks about the strangest things and gets angry if Jenny and her parents don't agree with her. Aunt Vivian says that the FBI is after her. She constantly writes letters to famous people, which is why, she claims, the FBI is so interested in her.

Sometimes she even thinks Jenny is talking with the FBI when she is on the phone with friends.

Jenny doesn't like to spend much time around her aunt, so she usually finds other things to do during her aunt's visits. Aunt Vivian is Jenny's mother's sister, and Jenny's mom gets nervous and moody when Aunt Vivian visits. Her mom gets angry with Jenny when she spends so much time at her friends' houses. But Jenny's not going to invite her friends over with her aunt acting so crazy!

Schizophrenia is a word that conjures up horrible thoughts and images—and it can be a horrible disease. But the more you understand about the disease, the less frightening it is. People are often secretive about this illness. Like most diseases, schizophrenia strikes many different kinds of people. In fact, 1 in 100 people in the United States have schizophrenia.

Life can be very, very difficult for people with schizophrenia. Schizophrenics' thinking is disturbed, which affects their behavior in many ways. They may speak oddly (it's hard to understand them), say things that don't make sense (for example, that the FBI is after them), or engage in strange behavior (like hiding out in their room all day). It is often difficult for a person with schizophrenia to participate in common activities. Schizophrenics often interpret events very differently from other people. For example, a person with schizophrenia may interpret a casual remark or a joke as a plot or threat against him or her.

Aunt Vivian really believes that the FBI is after her. This delusion is a condition of schizophrenia. Because she believes these things, she acts afraid much of the time. Aunt Vivian began writing letters to famous people 20 years ago when she saw a television show about a common country girl who married a famous movie star. She thought the TV show was sending her a personal message to contact all famous people. That idea is also a part of her disease.

Because life is complicated for someone with schizophrenia, caring about that person can be difficult, too. The best you can do is to understand the disease, so you don't take the person's strange behavior personally. You can learn how to live with the disease without being afraid or angry. You can learn to accept the person as he or she is. When you accept the mental illness, you know that the person acts a certain way because of the disease, not because of you. You can stop trying to cure the mentally ill person.

**Someone you know may have schizophrenia if he or she:**
- has had a noticeable change in behaviors
- expresses beliefs that have no basis in fact
- is increasingly agitated toward you and others
- says he or she hears voices
- has difficulty making sense
- believes that outside forces (like the Mafia or the FBI) are trying to control him or her

- keeps to him or herself
- acts frightened of others
- expresses the wrong emotion (laughs during a funeral, for example)
- is expressionless at times

Most people experience some of these symptoms at some time in their lives. But with schizophrenia the behaviors are severe, persistent, or recurrent. To someone with this disease, the world can be very lonely. Yet many people who have schizophrenia live happy lives. It is also important to know that with proper treatment, some people do recover from schizophrenia.

If you are worried about someone you know who may have schizophrenia, tell an adult you trust about your concerns. You can also talk to your family doctor or call the Alliance for the Mentally Ill in your area.

# CHAPTER THREE

# You and Your Family

If someone in your family has a mental illness, your home is probably chaotic sometimes. Promises may be broken, and some of your hopes may have been shattered. Family members might be confused about what to do, how to act, and what to say. Everyone may be hiding how they feel. Relationships have changed. Sometimes life seems to return to normal—and then another crisis occurs. You're never sure what to expect.

If someone in your family is mentally ill, you and your family have unique problems and challenges. You have special feelings and concerns. You might worry about the ill person harming himself or others, or you may feel threatened by this person. You might wonder if you have a mental illness, too. You probably want to know if your life will ever return to normal. These are all normal feelings and concerns.

## *Am I Crazy Too?*

Most teens who are close to someone with a mental illness—especially a family member—wonder if they, too, have a mental illness. They often feel a secret connection with the mentally ill relative and believe that the two of them are different from the rest of the family. When you spend a lot of time with someone who has mixed thoughts, talks about frightening topics, and acts oddly, you may begin to feel a little strange yourself. It is nice to have a close relationship with the mentally ill person—as long as you realize that you are two separate individuals with different thoughts and needs.

Even if you don't feel close to your mentally ill relative or friend, you might still worry whether you are also vulnerable to mental illness. It's easy to interpret feeling sad, lonely, or scared as a sign of mental illness. Everyone feels sad, scared, and lonely at times. But the symptoms of all mental illnesses are severe, persistent, or recurrent, and unless this is true for you, you do not have a mental illness.

It's hard being close to a mentally ill person, who thinks so differently from others. You might wonder if she holds some unique power; maybe God *is* talking to her, or the devil *is* trying to enter her brain. You may believe that if this can happen to her, it can happen to you.

Most likely, you do not have a mental illness. If mental illness runs in your family, however, you can take steps to keep yourself mentally healthy.

- Don't experiment with street drugs. Every drug, including cocaine, crack, marijuana, LSD, and alcohol—even beer or wine—interferes with the functioning of the brain and can cause permanent damage. Taking drugs is a dangerous risk—it's not worth it.
- Enjoy life without being involved with dangerous activities, such as climbing bridges that have been closed down, riding a motorcycle without a helmet, or speeding in a car. There are many fun things to do without putting yourself in danger.
- Stay involved with life. Get involved with friends and relatives. When things get rough, don't isolate yourself—reach out to others.

## *When You're Scared at Home*

Erica is afraid of her brother Doug. He has never hurt her, but his threats frighten her. One time he waved a garden hoe in her face. Erica locked herself in her room until her mother came home. By the time their mother returned, Doug was pacing back and forth in his bedroom. Their mother immediately realized that he was in trouble and called for help. Doug is in the hospital now. Erica feels bad that Doug is in the hospital. She thinks it might be her fault. She is caught between feeling afraid of her brother's behavior and feeling guilty that he has to be in the hospital. She wonders why he is so mean to her. She also feels responsible for protecting her mother, because Doug threatens her too. What can Erica or others do when someone threatens or becomes violent? How can Erica protect herself?

## *Keep Yourself Safe at All Times*

Not all mentally ill people become violent. But often because of their scary and illogical thinking, they think they're in danger and act threatening. Although much of a mentally ill person's bizarre behavior results from the disease, they are still responsible for their own behavior. The most important thing to remember is that you should never remain in a threatening situation.

Typically, people with mental illness strike out or threaten to hurt others for three reasons:

1. They believe they are in danger and strike out to protect themselves.
2. They are overly sensitive to what goes on around them and easily become defensive about and irritated with others' behaviors. For example, they may interpret your shutting a door loudly as an angry gesture.
3. They are hallucinating (seeing or hearing things that aren't there) and are responding to this sight or sound.

Try not to argue with someone whom you believe has mixed-up thoughts. Chances are, your argument will only aggravate the person more.

People with mental illness often feel angry because

of their low opinion of themselves. They feel hurt, embarrassed, and ashamed about their illness and may lash out in frustration at those closest to them. But no matter what the reason for their behavior, your safety comes first. If you are scared for your life or afraid of being hurt, leave the house and get help. Always put your own safety first.

## *Understanding Your Many Feelings*

People who have a friend or relative with a mental illness have many feelings in common. Here are a few of the most common reactions we have when we find out that someone we care about has a mental illness.

Sadness/Grief—about the loss of the person as he or she was before the illness, about lost plans and expectations, because someone you care about is in pain.

Confusion—about what is happening, about why someone gets mental illness, about what to do.

Anger—because the person has changed and family relationships have changed, because the person doesn't seem to want to get better, because others aren't doing what you had expected.

Fear—that you too may have a mental illness, that life will never return to normal, that you may have to take responsibility for the mentally ill person, that the mentally ill person will harm himself or herself or others.

Guilt—because you're healthy and someone you care

about is ill, because you think it could just as easily be you with mental illness, because you feel like you did something wrong that contributed to the illness, because you feel you should be doing more to help the person get better.

**Anxiety/Nervousness**—because things seem so unpredictable; you are not quite sure what's going to happen next.

**Jealousy**—that the mentally ill person is getting so much attention.

**Acceptance**—of the ill person's condition and the changes this created for you and for him or her.

**Hope**—because you can accept the way things are and feel encouraged about the future.

It is all right to have these feelings. Feelings are not right or wrong; they just are. It's not wrong to be angry or jealous; it is natural that you would have such feelings. It doesn't mean that you have to act on these feelings. You do need to share them with someone, however. Sometimes when we feel fearful, jealous, or hurt, we try to "get even" by hurting those we think hurt us. Or we withdraw and keep to ourselves. But when we get even or withdraw, we don't allow others to give us love and attention, because our anger or aloofness pushes them away.

### Kim Always Keeps a Smile on Her Face

Kim's sister Kathy is in the hospital with schizophrenia. Kim and her parents visit Kathy a couple of times a month. When Kim is alone with Kathy, sometimes Kathy rambles on and on about things that happened in the past, while other times she won't say a word. But Kim always keeps a smile on her face. She wants to visit Kathy, but she hates going to the hospital. She feels sick to her stomach when she's there, and once she almost fainted. But she didn't tell anyone. Why should she? Her parents feel bad enough.

It is not until Kim leaves the hospital and is alone that she cries. Sometimes she cries for hours until she falls asleep or her throat gets sore. She feels worse on the days her friends have something special planned, like going to the beach or the fair, and she misses out on it. She doesn't tell them she's going to visit Kathy in the hospital. Kim hardly ever talks about Kathy to anyone.

It is important to let others know how you feel, including the mentally ill person, your parents, and your friends. Don't hide your sadness. Of course you are sad to see your friend or family member in the hospital. Don't pretend you're happy when you're not. Practice letting others know how you feel and what you want. Kim would feel better, less alone, if she would open up to someone about her feelings.

## *What Are You Going to Do about How You Feel?*

What can you do about your feelings of guilt? Some guilt is healthy, like when you feel bad about lying to a friend. But maybe you feel guilty about things that are outside of your control. We can't change what has already happened—and we can't make someone get well. What is important is to understand how you feel about it. What are you feeling? Listen to your feelings. Whatever you are feeling—hurt, anxious, angry, excited, cheated, or guilty—accept these emotions.

After you take the time to recognize and accept how you feel, decide what you are going to do about how you feel. Don't respond blindly to your feelings. Decide which is the best way to respond. Then talk to someone about your feelings.

### My Parents Ignore Me

Ever since Becky's sister Judy got sick, her parents have ignored her. Becky feels like nothing else matters to them. Becky's older sister, Judy, was hospitalized three years ago, two days before Becky turned 14. Since then, life for Becky and her family has changed. Becky feels more alone and sad. She doesn't like spending time at home much. Before Judy got sick, their parents would brag about Becky and Judy's accomplishments, but not anymore. Recently Becky brought home a project she got an "A" on, and nobody mentioned it at the dinner table. Dinner is quiet now, as if being still can prevent Judy from getting sicker.

Becky has not told her parents about her feelings, because she is worried about them. She thinks she will burden her parents if she tells them she's unhappy —and they already have Judy to worry about. Becky wonders if her parents love her. One time she thought about getting sick or in some kind of accident so she could get all the attention. For now she chooses to spend most of her time at her friend's house, where she feels safe and comfortable.

Becky's experience is common among families in which a brother, sister, or parent has a mental illness. Too often the well parent(s) focuses attention on the ill person. At least two choices are available to Becky, though. She can continue spending time at her friend's house. A safe place where we are welcomed and cared for is a good place to go.

Becky may also want to try to talk with her parents about her feelings and concerns. Perhaps her parents don't know that Becky is hurt about what is happening at home. They may assume that everything is OK because she hasn't said anything. When parents are busy trying to care for a mentally ill loved one, sometimes they need an extra nudge to give you the attention you deserve. For Becky, telling her parents how she feels may give them the chance to show her how they really feel—how much they love her.

## *My Friends All Have Normal Families*

"Sometimes I wish I had another family." This is a common wish among those who live with someone with mental illness. Many people think that they are the only one whose parents have divorced, whose father has gone into treatment for alcoholism, or whose brother is mentally ill. This is not true. Many families have a member with a mental illness. It just seems like other families are "normal" because most people keep things like mental illness, divorce, and alcoholism a secret. But they don't have to be secrets.

# CHAPTER FOUR
# What You Can Do

We all have many expectations about life. Each day we anticipate how our day will proceed—even particular events—and how people will act in a certain situation. But sometimes things change and what we expect and what we get are different. For example, you may have expected to play first base in your softball game, but when you arrived at the practice game, the coach had chosen someone else for first base and put you in the outfield. Maybe you felt angry and disappointed—but would you leave the game angry, or stay and play? Life does not always meet all our expectations—that's just the way life is.

Schizophrenia, depression, or any other mental illness is not an experience we expect or want in our lives, or in the lives of those we love. You find that your relative or friend behaves differently since the illness, which probably upsets and angers you. But do you have to end the relationship, or can you learn new ways of relating to this person? Although the person has changed, you may still be able to have a very special relationship with him or her—a relationship you can even enjoy. But you must be willing to change your expectations of what can happen between the two of you. The relationship you have with the mentally ill person depends on how ill the person is. Some people with schizophrenia are so sick they can't talk well enough to make sense. Other people are so depressed they stay in bed all day.

Understanding the expectations we place on ourselves, our families, and the ill person can help us accept things the way they are—even when they are different from what we had hoped for. Here are some examples of expectations that most often cause hurt and anger:

- "If only my friend would talk more, he would feel better."
- "I expect my mother to be more fun when she comes to watch me play football. But she just sits there and doesn't cheer me on."
- "If my dad really loved me, he wouldn't be in the hospital on my birthday."
- "My mother expects me to spend more time with my sister, but I don't want to."
- "I hate going to school! Nothing is ever how I want it to be."

- "I should visit my grandfather when he is in the hospital, even though I don't really like him."
- "I should spend more time with my friend. Maybe then she would get better."

When we keep expecting one thing and getting another, or when we expect too much of ourselves, we end up feeling hurt, disappointed, and angry. If you kept showing up to play first base but always played in the outfield, you would most likely feel upset at every game. On the other hand, if you accepted that you might not play first base every time, you wouldn't be as angry or hurt. It isn't wrong that you want to play first base—it's just not what the coach decided. You may even discover you like playing the outfield better.

What are your expectations of yourself, your family, and your friends? Do you keep wanting things to go one way and then they go another? What expectations can you change so you won't be angry or hurt every time? What do you need to accept in yourself and others to make life less painful for you?

Try to begin a new relationship with the mentally ill person based on what you now understand about the disease. The person's capabilities are not as good as they once were. With this new understanding, change your expectations and begin a new relationship.

## *Talk to Someone You Trust*

Debbie worries that if she tells her friends that her mother has depression, they'll start looking at her strangely. Not too many people know about her mother's problems. But sometimes Debbie wishes she could tell others about it. It's hard keeping it a secret all the time.

Like Debbie, many people treat mental illness like a big horrible secret. Perhaps your parents keep a family member's mental illness a secret, so you think you must, too. Or you may be afraid of what others might think of you if you tell them about your family member or close friend who has a mental illness.

Keeping mental illness a secret only makes it more of a problem. Choose someone to talk about your thoughts and concerns with—a friend, neighbor, relative, parent, teacher, school counselor, or grandparent. You're not alone. Others do understand. If your relative or friend had cancer you wouldn't be embarrassed to talk about it with others. Mental illness is another disease. You will find that your problems get smaller the more you open up.

## *Try This Exercise*

On a piece of paper, write out three things you would really like someone to understand about you or your family. Then choose two people you would like to tell these things. Pick one adult and one friend. You may have never done this before, so it may seem scary. But give it a try—something wonderful will happen. There will be two more people in the world who understand you.

You can also try this exercise with three questions

you have about the mental illness, yourself, or your family.

Every family has its ups and downs. Every family has troubles. All we need to do is end the secrecy—to stop pretending everything's "perfect." We are all doing the best we can. If your parents ignore you, they probably don't mean to. They are just doing the best they can with what they know. Most likely, they never learned to open up about their feelings either. But you can. Let them know how you feel and what you need. Start asking those questions you have kept to yourself. Why wait any longer?

## *Talking to Your Family*

Often it is hardest to talk to those we love the most. We are afraid that what we say will make them angry, or that they won't care about what we have to say and then we will be hurt. Many families don't know how to sit down together and talk to each other, especially about problems and concerns. Is there something you would really like to talk to your parents about? Do you have something to say to your sister or brother or grandparent? Most likely, you want to talk to them about the changes in your life because of your friend or relative's mental illness.

Don't wait for others to ask you to open up. It may never happen unless you start. Others care what you think and feel, but they may never have learned how to talk about these things. They are probably worried about how you might respond.

Your parents don't have all the answers. Sometimes they don't know what to do. They certainly can't predict the future, or guarantee that everything will be all right. No one has all the answers about mental illness—we all need to be patient and understanding as we learn to live with this disease.

## Talking with God

It may help you to talk with God. God can be your invisible and powerful friend. You may find it difficult at first to talk with God, to ask God for help. Talk to God about your family, about the mentally ill person, about your feelings. You may discover you feel less lonely and can handle difficult times. You can even tell God about the times you miss or enjoy—and pray for better times.

## When Are We Going on a Vacation?

Too often families with a mentally ill member get too serious. One 14-year-old said that once her mother became ill with depression, the family never went on vacations. If your family is like that, make time for yourself to have fun. Go on mini-vacations over to a friend's house. Perhaps you can go on a trip with a neighbor or relative. When you are invited to go on a vacation with someone you enjoy and trust, go! You deserve to have a good time, to enjoy yourself. Although it is too bad that your mentally ill relative can't do as much as he or she used to do, you don't have to stop having fun.

### *Keep a Diary—Write a Letter*

Many teens find it helpful to write to someone about what is going on in their lives. You could write to a friend who moved away who understands and cares about you. You might want to write a favorite aunt or uncle about what is going on in your life. Some of us like to write in a journal or diary. Others like writing letters to God, keeping them in a journal. Writing helps release our feelings and concerns.

Writing letters that you don't actually send to someone can make it easier when you do reach out to this person. Write a letter but don't send it; then talk to the person when you are ready. Claire writes letters to her mentally ill sister, even though they live together. When Claire is angry with her sister, she writes an "angry letter." She says it really helps get her feelings out. Later she can talk more calmly to her sister about why she is angry or hurt.

### *Keep Your Dreams*

Walter grew up on a farm. There were many chores to do after school. Walter had to do more than most teenagers, because his younger brother, Jeff, didn't do much work. When Jeff came home from school, many times he would hide in the barn above where the cows were fed instead of finishing his chores. Walter knew his brother was up there, because dust fell down as he milked the cows. The brothers didn't speak to one another during this time. Walter just left Jeff alone. But he was worried about him. Jeff didn't have any friends. Walter heard some of the other kids at school whispering about Jeff. Walter hoped that if he finished Jeff's chores and kept quiet, sooner or later Jeff would snap out of it. But Jeff never seemed to get any better. As he got older, he withdrew more.

Jeff and Walter's parents were too busy with their own chores to notice much change in Jeff. Jeff had always been quiet, and his doing poorly in school didn't bother them. They hoped both sons would take over the farm someday. Walter never brought up his concerns to them, and they never asked.

When the school coach encouraged Walter to join the football team, he declined. Although he loved football, he couldn't keep up with football practice and also do Jeff's work. During his senior year, Walter's English teacher told him that he was a good writer and asked him to help write the school newspaper. This made Walter proud, and he thought about how exciting it would be to become a newspaper reporter someday. He turned down the offer, though, since he didn't have time to work on the paper. Besides, he thought, why should I dream about what could be when I know I have to stay on the farm and take care of my brother?

Walter is now 33. His parents have since died. The farm wasn't bringing in enough money, so it had to be sold. Jeff, now 26, is in a treatment program that helps mentally ill adults live on their own. Jeff doesn't need to live with Walter. Walter is not sure what to do now. He never thought he would do anything but take care of the farm and Jeff. Walter is confused and sad.

Now Walter must think about what he wants to do with his life. He needs to learn how to dream. Until he starts dreaming, his life will seem empty. Maybe he'll dream about writing—about becoming a sportswriter, perhaps. Maybe he could go to college and eventually teach agriculture, or he could become a salesman, or—who knows? No one will know until he starts dreaming.

It is important to keep your dreams and plans alive, even when someone you care about seems to have lost his or hers. Putting off your dreams and plans won't help anyone get better. Start dreaming now about what you want to become. If you are asked to join a team or do a special project, say yes. Dream about all the possibilities your future holds for you— there are so many!

## *Take Good Care of Yourself*

Brad feels guilty that he is well and his sister, Chris, is sick and unhappy. He doesn't want to tell her if he's had a good day. He kept it a secret when he received an award in gym class. He thought he shouldn't brag in front of her. He didn't even tell his parents, because they seem so preoccupied with Chris. Brad thinks they want him to be quiet about things like that, because Chris would feel worse if she knew.

When we care about someone with a mental illness or any disease, it's easy to put our own health and dreams aside while we try to help that person. But you can care about a mentally ill person and still take good care of yourself. The best thing we can do for someone else is to stay healthy ourselves. If we are unhealthy and unhappy, we won't have much to offer others. If we forget to dream, we may wake up one day unsure of what we want to do.

Here are some simple ways to make sure you are taking good care of yourself:

- Talk with your friends about what is going on with you—tell them about the person you care about who has a mental illness.
- Keep up your interests. If you have enjoyed playing basketball or taking dance lessons after school, continue doing these things. Stopping what you enjoy isn't going to help anyone else get better.
- Be realistic about what you can do with the mentally ill person. Don't spend too much time with him or her if it is painful or stressful for you. It's better to spend short, enjoyable times with someone than to stretch it out because you feel guilty.
- Keep talking about your feelings and your thoughts to others. Don't withdraw—reach out.
- Find people and places that you enjoy and where you can feel safe. It's all right to spend time away from home if your home is threatening or too chaotic. But don't hide out alone—be with others whom you care about.

- Experimenting with alcohol and drugs is very dangerous, especially if there is mental illness in the family. Find friends who don't take drugs or drink alcohol, including beer and wine.
- Keep your dreams active in your mind.

Don't give up hope. Hope is believing that someday a cure for mental illness may be found. Hope is believing that you can make a positive change in your life. Hope is something you can share with others.

## *Letting Go*

Everyone must learn to let go of things in their lives. We have to let go of people who move away, clothes we've outgrown, and expectations that aren't realistic. Letting go means that you stop trying to take care of everything and everybody. We let go of trying to cure the person of his or her mental illness. Letting go means loving people without feeling responsible for their happiness. It means accepting the mentally ill person as he or she is—with the disease. To let go is to spend time with the mentally ill person, but not more time than feels right to you.

You can let go of worry, guilt, and anger. The only way to accept the mentally ill person and your life as it is today is to let go of how it was yesterday—to let go of wishing it were yesterday or wishing things were different. Then you can make room in your life for something new: new dreams, expectations, and relationships.

# CHAPTER FIVE
# Happy Endings

How well you learn to take care of yourself now will determine what kind of adult you will become. If you start to withdraw from others and not open up and talk, for example, you may find yourself a very lonely adult. At the same time, you don't want to get into relationships in which you are always taking care of others. It's important to learn to care for others without feeling obligated to do everything for them. You can learn to enjoy your life, even if disruption is sometimes a part of it, and to accept what you cannot change.

Finding joy in life can be difficult when someone you care about is in so much pain. It is possible, however. Here are three stories of people who care about someone with mental illness—and who can tell about their happy endings.

### Jeannie's Brother Karl

Jeannie's brother Karl changed drastically when he was about 17. All of a sudden he isolated himself, stopped playing with Jeannie, and seemed angry most of the time. He dropped out of school and started hanging out in an abandoned building down the street. Other kids who didn't go to school either hung out there too. Jeannie knew they were drinking alcohol and smoking pot. She thought she smelled marijuana on Karl when he came home at night. Jeannie was frightened. She missed her brother—the one who used to have long talks with her after school. She hesitated to tell her parents, though, because they were having a lot of fights lately and she didn't want to make things worse.

But Karl was acting stranger every day. He came into her room one afternoon and really scared her by telling her that the house was being invaded by evil spirits! She thought this could be true—after all, everything at home was changing for the worse. She finally decided to tell her best friend, Carrie, about what was going on. Jeannie was a little worried what Carrie might think, but Jeannie wanted someone to know what was happening. Carrie told her that it sounded like Karl needed help and that she should talk to her parents or the school counselor.

Jeannie decided instead to talk to her Aunt Susan. Her aunt was happy that Jeannie had confided in her and offered to talk to Jeannie's mother. Soon, Jeannie's mother sat down with her and listened to what she had to say. As a family, they decided to take Karl to the hospital for an evaluation. There they learned that he had schizophrenia and further treatment in the hospital would be necessary.

Karl spent two months in the hospital. He stopped smoking marijuana and now takes a medication that helps regulate his thoughts. He hasn't returned to the person Jeannie once knew, and the hospital staff warned her that he may have this disease all his life. The family is setting up a plan to get him into a treatment program that helps people like Karl finish school and learn to live on their own. Jeannie misses the brother who used to be so playful—but she's happy to see him doing so much better. She hopes that they will be able to have some good talks again.

### Mary's Story

Mary never knew that her mother had manic depression. She didn't realize that when her mother was creative, energetic, and talkative, she was manic. During those times, her mother would do things with the kids, join one or several groups at church, volunteer for some cause, and keep the house clean. At other times, Mary's mother had little or no energy, stayed in bed, and seemed to cry about the smallest things. During these times, Mary's mother was experiencing depression. Mary's mom would drop out of the activities and groups she was involved in, do very little with the kids, and didn't help clean the house.

Mary had thought this was normal behavior for mothers. But when her mom cried so often, Mary would feel sad and guilty herself, as if she were somehow making her mother unhappy. Mary didn't like to see her mom get so involved in something, only to withdraw from it later. One time her mom made elaborate plans to take Mary and three of her friends on a vacation to Canada. Everyone was really excited. About a week before the trip, Mary's mom said she just couldn't go—she didn't have the energy. Mary had to call her friends and tell them the trip was cancelled. She was very embarrassed and hurt. She wanted to yell at her mother, but she also felt bad that her mom was sick again.

Mary didn't know her mother had manic depression until Mary left home at the age of 21 to attend college. In her psychology class, she read a book called *Moodswing*, which described people who sounded just like her mother. She read about lithium, a drug that helps people with manic depression. Mary sat down and wrote a long letter to her mother, telling her what it was like growing up and that she believed her mother had manic depression. Mary knew that her mother might get angry and reject what the letter said, but she wrote it anyway. She also told her mother how much she loved her and hoped she could be happy.

At first her mother was angry and hurt. No one wants to believe that they have a mental illness. But soon after she received the letter, she began feeling depressed again. This time she decided she wanted to stop feeling so tired and sad, so she sat down and read the book that Mary had read. About a week later, Mary's mother visited a psychiatrist. The psychiatrist suggested she get counseling and prescribed lithium.

It's been two years now, and Mary's mother no longer has severe mood swings like she used to. Mary and her mother talk regularly on the phone. Mary meets with a group of other young adults who grew up with a mentally ill parent. The group has helped her deal with the many feelings she has had about her mother and the disease.

Not everyone responds so well to medication, nor is everyone willing to get treatment when told they have a mental illness. Fortunately for Mary and her mother, they were willing to get help for themselves—and they both are happier because of it.

### Ricky's Friend

Ricky and Van were very good friends. They sat next to each other in homeroom at Cleveland High School because their last names both began with T—Ricky Taylor and Van Tanner. They took long bike rides, walked to school together, played basketball, and sneaked out of their windows at night to meet at their secret fort.

In their sophomore year, Ricky and Van tried some drugs at a party they attended together. The effects of the drug scared Van. He didn't like how the marijuana and the pill he took made him feel. Ricky enjoyed the high and wanted to do more, however. A few days after the party, Ricky found someone he could buy marijuana and other drugs from. Ricky began getting high every day. He wanted Van to get high with him and teased Van for being so scared. Ricky began skipping school and missing most of his classes. Van was worried about Ricky, but he didn't know what he could do. Soon they lost contact with one another. Ricky found friends who would get high with him and Van stayed away from Ricky.

After about a year, Ricky called Van one night very late. Ricky was talking very strangely. He said voices were telling him that his parents were trying to kill him. He told Van, "Something is taking over my brain." Van was scared. He thought that Ricky was probably high on some drug. Finally Van told Ricky to try to get some sleep and they could talk tomorrow.

When Van called Ricky's house the following day, his parents told him that Ricky was in the hospital. "What for?" Van asked. "Ricky is in the hospital because he has a mental illness called schizophrenia," Ricky's mother said. "The doctors say that he'll have to remain for treatment for at least a month." Van was frightened. He learned that Ricky had started showing signs of the disease about six months before. Van felt awful. He thought he should have known that Ricky was in trouble and he should have told someone. But that would have been snitching, and friends don't snitch. But he wished he had snitched—then maybe Ricky wouldn't be in the hospital!

Ricky stayed in the hospital for a month and then entered a treatment program for people who have a mental illness and abuse drugs. Van was told that this would be a difficult time for Ricky. Ricky would have to stay off drugs and work hard with the treatment staff to get better. They told Van that Ricky might have schizophrenia forever.

Van visits Ricky at the treatment program about once a week. It's hard for him to see his friend struggling so hard. They don't do the same things they used to do and they talk a lot less. Van has decided that he can only do so much for Ricky. He's also decided to stay friends with him. Van found out that he couldn't have stopped Ricky from getting schizophrenia or from taking drugs. He also decided that it is OK to tell on friends if they are abusing drugs. Van and Ricky are planning a short bike trip this coming weekend. Not everything has changed because of Ricky's schizophrenia. The friends still like to ride bikes together.

A happy ending doesn't mean that everything happens exactly like we wish it would. Happy endings do include you. Happy endings mean that you can continue on with your life and still have a relationship with your mentally ill relative or friend, if you choose.

# How Are You Doing?

Which of these statements are true for you?

1. I do *not* abuse drugs or alcohol.
2. I do things I enjoy which are not hurtful to me or others or harmful to myself or others' property.
3. I can spend relaxed or playful time at home.
4. Most of the time I do not worry about the mentally ill person.
5. I have at least two friends whom I see or talk with regularly.
6. I feel safe at home.
7. On days I have off, I can get up before 11:00 A.M., I have energy, and I can work or have fun.
8. I have done something in the last year that I am proud of.
9. I tell others about how I feel when I am upset or happy about something.
10. I talk to others about the mental illness and how it affects me.
11. When a parent or friend tries to talk with me or show they care, I listen to what they have to say and am able to let them know I care, too.
12. I feel secure that, overall, everything will work out for the best.

The more of these statements that are true for you, the better you are doing. If you find yourself saying that five or more of these statements are not true, try to find someone that you can talk to. Nothing is wrong with you, and you are not a bad person. Life has become too complicated and painful for you, though. You need someone to help you take better care of yourself. All of us need others to help and understand us. Talk to someone now—don't wait. If you wait, you will find that when you are an adult, you will still need someone to talk to, only it will be harder for you to find that person and open up because you have waited so long.

# Where to Look for Help

The Eight Stage Program
Julie Tallard Johnson
P.O. Box 19067
Minneapolis, MN 55419
(612) 872-1565

   Resources, information, and workshops on how mental illness affects families.

National Depressive and
Manic Depressive Association
Merchandise Mart
Box 3395
Chicago, IL 60654
(312) 939-2442

   Resources and groups for families.

National Alliance for the Mentally Ill
2101 Wilson Boulevard
Suite 302
Arlington, VA 22201
(703) 524-7600

   Information and groups for families of the mentally ill.

Youth Emotions Anonymous
P.O. Box 4245
St. Paul, MN 55104
(612) 647-9712

   A program for youths ages 13 to 19 to gain better emotional health.

## Videos

*After the Tears: Teens Talk About Mental Illness in Their Families.*
Produced by United Mental Health, Inc.
1945 Fifth Avenue
Pittsburgh, PA 15219

## Books

### Fiction

Hyland, Betty. *The Girl with the Crazy Brother.* New York: Franklin Watts, 1987. Enjoyable, readable story for young people who have family members with mental illness.

Naylor, Phyllis Reynolds. *The Keeper.* New York: Bantam Books, 1986. A worthwhile book for teenagers who are living with a mentally ill loved one or who want to understand how a mentally ill friend lives.

Riley, Jocelyn. *Crazy Quilt.* New York: Bantam Books, 1986. An account of a girl whose mother has a mental illness.

———. *Only My Mouth Is Smiling.* New York: William Morrow & Co., 1986. A powerful story of how a girl with a mentally ill mother learns to act as if she's happy. She puts on a happy face for others, but inside she is in pain.

## Nonfiction

Burns, David. *Feeling Good: The New Mood Therapy.* New York: William Morrow & Co., 1980. Outlines an effective treatment program for depression.

Fieve, R.R., M.D. *Moodswing.* New York: Bantam Books, 1975. A very readable book on manic depression and people in history who have been affected.

Johnson, Julie Tallard. *Hidden Victims: An Eight-Stage Healing Process for Families and Friends of the Mentally Ill.* New York: Doubleday & Co., 1988. Help in dealing with a loved one's mental illness. Offers hope and guidance to anyone who cares about someone with a mental illness.

Kolehmainen, Janet, and Sandra Handwerk. *Teen Suicide.* Minneapolis: Lerner Publications, 1986. Offers advice on preventing and coping with suicide.

McGuire, Paula. *Putting It Together.* New York: Delacorte Press, 1987. Interviews with children, teenagers, and counselors about the effects of family breakups.

Sheehan, Susan. *Is There No Place on Earth for Me?* New York: Vintage Books, 1983. The story of one woman's experience living with schizophrenia.

Torrey, E. Fuller. *Surviving Schizophrenia: A Family Manual.* New York: Harper & Row, 1988. Offers advice and help to families with a schizophrenic member.

Zerafa, Judy. *Go For It.* New York: Workman Publishing Co., 1982. Offers advice to teens on how to improve relationships and gain control over one's life.

# Index

---

**Learn how to cope with other modern problems in**

Eating Disorders
A Question and Answer Book
About Anorexia Nervosa
and Bulimia Nervosa
by Ellen Erlanger

Feeling Safe, Feeling Strong
How to Avoid Sexual Abuse and
What to Do If It Happens to You
by Susan Neiburg Terkel
and Janice E. Rench

Teen Pregnancy
by Sonia Bowe-Gutman

Teen Sexuality
Decisions and Choices
by Janice E. Rench

Teen Suicide
A Book for Friends, Family,
and Classmates
by Janet Kolehmainen
and Sandra Handwerk

Understanding AIDS
by Ethan A. Lerner, M.D., Ph.D.

SPANISH EDITION:
Comprendiendo el SIDA
by Ethan A. Lerner, M.D., Ph.D.